Go Play!

by Giulia Verzariu
illustrated by Diane Paterson

Pre-Decodable 6

Mc Graw Hill Education

Bothell, WA • Chicago, IL • Columbus, OH • New York, NY

MHEonline.com

Send all inquiries to:
McGraw-Hill Education
8787 Orion Place
Columbus, OH 43240

ISBN: 978-0-02-145108-1
MHID: 0-02-145108-7

Printed in China

9 10 11 12 13 DSS 28 27 26 25 24

Go  !

run

Go  a  !

kick ball

Go  a !

up swing

Go  down a  slide!

Go  a 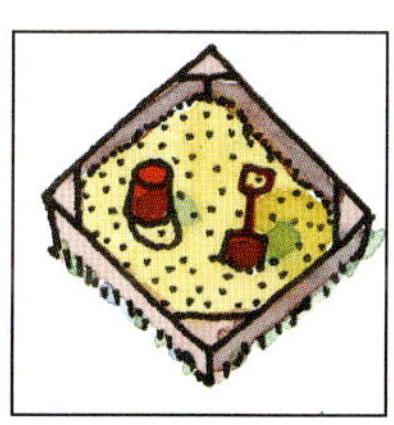!

dig sandbox

Go  !

play